50 Indian Curry Creation Recipes for Home

By: Kelly Johnson

Table of Contents

- Chicken Tikka Masala
- Butter Chicken (Murgh Makhani)
- Lamb Rogan Josh
- Chana Masala (Chickpea Curry)
- Palak Paneer (Spinach and Cottage Cheese Curry)
- Dal Makhani
- Aloo Gobi (Potato and Cauliflower Curry)
- Baingan Bharta (Roasted Eggplant Curry)
- Fish Curry
- Goan Prawn Curry
- Rajma Masala (Kidney Bean Curry)
- Malai Kofta (Vegetable Dumplings in Creamy Tomato Sauce)
- Kadai Chicken
- Bhindi Masala (Okra Curry)
- Matar Paneer (Peas and Cottage Cheese Curry)
- Keema Curry (Minced Meat Curry)
- Dhansak (Parsi Lentil and Meat Curry)
- Chicken Korma
- Vegetable Jalfrezi
- Mushroom Masala
- Achari Chicken (Pickled Spiced Chicken)
- Baingan Mirch Ka Salan (Eggplant and Chili Curry)
- Methi Chicken (Fenugreek Chicken Curry)
- Lauki Kofta (Bottle Gourd Dumplings in Tomato Gravy)
- Hyderabadi Biryani
- Prawn Masala
- Paneer Butter Masala
- Chicken Saagwala (Chicken in Spinach Sauce)
- Aloo Methi (Potato and Fenugreek Curry)
- Sindhi Kadhi
- Keema Matar (Minced Meat with Peas)
- Chicken Vindaloo
- Tomato Pappu (Tomato Lentil Curry)
- Nihari
- Gatte Ki Sabzi (Gram Flour Dumplings in Yogurt Gravy)

- Chicken Chettinad
- Baingan Patiala (Eggplant in Tomato Onion Gravy)
- Murgh Do Pyaza (Chicken with Double Onions)
- Methi Malai Murg (Fenugreek Cream Chicken)
- Khumb Matar (Mushroom and Peas Curry)
- Chicken Kolhapuri
- Palak Kofta Curry (Spinach Dumplings in Tomato Gravy)
- Dal Tadka
- Shahi Paneer
- Malabar Fish Curry
- Punjabi Kadhi Pakora
- Mutton Curry
- Kerala Style Paneer Roast
- Chicken Malai Curry
- Aloo Posto (Potatoes in Poppy Seed Paste)

Chicken Tikka Masala

Ingredients:

For the Chicken Tikka:

- 1.5 pounds boneless, skinless chicken thighs or breasts, cut into bite-sized pieces
- 1 cup plain yogurt
- 1 tablespoon ginger-garlic paste
- 1 tablespoon garam masala
- 1 tablespoon ground cumin
- 1 tablespoon ground coriander
- 1 teaspoon turmeric
- 1 teaspoon chili powder (adjust to taste)
- 1 teaspoon smoked paprika (for color)
- Salt and black pepper to taste
- 2 tablespoons vegetable oil

For the Masala Sauce:

- 2 tablespoons vegetable oil
- 1 large onion, finely chopped
- 3 cloves garlic, minced
- 1 tablespoon ginger, minced
- 1 teaspoon ground cumin
- 1 teaspoon ground coriander
- 1 teaspoon turmeric
- 1 teaspoon chili powder
- 1 teaspoon paprika
- 1 can (14 oz) crushed tomatoes
- 1 cup heavy cream
- Salt and sugar to taste
- Fresh cilantro for garnish (optional)

Instructions:

In a bowl, combine yogurt, ginger-garlic paste, garam masala, cumin, coriander, turmeric, chili powder, smoked paprika, salt, and black pepper. Mix well.
Add the chicken pieces to the marinade, ensuring each piece is well-coated.
Marinate for at least 2 hours or overnight in the refrigerator.
Preheat your grill or oven to high heat. Thread the marinated chicken pieces onto skewers and grill or bake until fully cooked with a nice char on the edges.
In a large skillet, heat vegetable oil over medium heat. Add chopped onions and sauté until they become translucent.
Add minced garlic and ginger to the onions and sauté for an additional 1-2 minutes.
Stir in ground cumin, ground coriander, turmeric, chili powder, and paprika. Cook the spices for about 1 minute to enhance their flavors.
Pour in the crushed tomatoes and cook the mixture for 5-7 minutes, allowing the tomatoes to break down.
Add the grilled chicken pieces to the tomato mixture and stir to coat the chicken with the sauce.
Pour in the heavy cream and stir well. Simmer the sauce for an additional 10-15 minutes, allowing it to thicken.
Adjust the seasoning with salt and sugar to taste.
Garnish with fresh cilantro if desired.
Serve the Chicken Tikka Masala hot over rice or with naan bread.

Enjoy this classic Indian dish with its tender and flavorful chicken pieces immersed in a luscious and creamy tomato-based sauce.

Butter Chicken (Murgh Makhani)

Ingredients:

For the Marination:

- 1.5 pounds boneless, skinless chicken thighs or breasts, cut into bite-sized pieces
- 1 cup plain yogurt
- 1 tablespoon ginger-garlic paste
- 1 teaspoon ground turmeric
- 1 teaspoon ground cumin
- 1 teaspoon chili powder
- 1 teaspoon garam masala
- Salt and black pepper to taste

For the Sauce:

- 3 tablespoons unsalted butter
- 1 large onion, finely chopped
- 3 cloves garlic, minced
- 1 tablespoon ginger, minced
- 1 teaspoon ground cumin
- 1 teaspoon ground coriander
- 1 teaspoon chili powder
- 1 teaspoon paprika
- 1 can (14 oz) crushed tomatoes
- 1 cup heavy cream
- 1 tablespoon sugar
- Salt to taste
- Fresh cilantro for garnish

Instructions:

In a bowl, combine yogurt, ginger-garlic paste, ground turmeric, ground cumin, chili powder, garam masala, salt, and black pepper. Mix well.

Add the chicken pieces to the marinade, ensuring each piece is well-coated.
Marinate for at least 2 hours or overnight in the refrigerator.
Preheat your oven to broil or grill the chicken on a barbecue.
Thread the marinated chicken pieces onto skewers and grill or broil until fully cooked with a nice char on the edges.
In a large skillet, melt butter over medium heat. Add chopped onions and sauté until they become translucent.
Add minced garlic and ginger to the onions and sauté for an additional 1-2 minutes.
Stir in ground cumin, ground coriander, chili powder, and paprika. Cook the spices for about 1 minute to enhance their flavors.
Pour in the crushed tomatoes and cook the mixture for 5-7 minutes, allowing the tomatoes to break down.
Add the grilled chicken pieces to the tomato mixture and stir to coat the chicken with the sauce.
Pour in the heavy cream and stir well. Simmer the sauce for an additional 10-15 minutes, allowing it to thicken.
Add sugar and salt to taste.
Garnish with fresh cilantro.
Serve the Butter Chicken hot over rice or with naan bread.

Enjoy this indulgent and creamy Butter Chicken with its tender, flavorful chicken pieces in a rich and aromatic tomato-based sauce.

Lamb Rogan Josh

Ingredients:

- 2 pounds boneless lamb, cut into bite-sized pieces
- 3 tablespoons vegetable oil or ghee
- 2 large onions, finely chopped
- 3 cloves garlic, minced
- 1 tablespoon ginger, minced
- 1 cup plain yogurt, whisked
- 1 cup tomato puree
- 2 teaspoons ground coriander
- 2 teaspoons ground cumin
- 1 teaspoon turmeric powder
- 1 teaspoon paprika
- 1 teaspoon ground cinnamon
- 1 teaspoon ground cardamom
- 1 teaspoon ground cloves
- 2 teaspoons ground fennel seeds
- 1 teaspoon Kashmiri red chili powder (adjust to taste)
- Salt to taste
- 1 cup water
- Fresh cilantro for garnish

Instructions:

In a large bowl, combine the lamb pieces with yogurt, ground coriander, ground cumin, turmeric, paprika, ground cinnamon, ground cardamom, ground cloves, ground fennel seeds, and Kashmiri red chili powder. Mix well and let it marinate for at least 2 hours, preferably overnight.
In a large, heavy-bottomed pot, heat the oil or ghee over medium heat.
Add the chopped onions and sauté until they become golden brown.
Add minced garlic and ginger to the onions, and sauté for an additional 1-2 minutes until the raw smell disappears.
Add the marinated lamb to the pot and brown the meat on all sides.
Pour in the tomato puree and stir well to combine with the lamb.
Add salt to taste and continue to cook for another 5 minutes.
Pour in the water, bring the mixture to a boil, and then reduce the heat to low.

Cover the pot and simmer for 1.5 to 2 hours or until the lamb is tender and the flavors are well blended. Stir occasionally.
Adjust salt and spices to taste.
Garnish with fresh cilantro before serving.
Serve the Lamb Rogan Josh hot, paired with steamed rice or naan bread.

Enjoy the rich and aromatic flavors of this traditional Kashmiri dish, Lamb Rogan Josh, which showcases the intricate blend of spices and slow-cooked tenderness of the lamb.

Chana Masala (Chickpea Curry)

Ingredients:

- 2 cans (15 oz each) chickpeas, drained and rinsed (or 3 cups cooked chickpeas)
- 2 tablespoons vegetable oil
- 1 large onion, finely chopped
- 3 cloves garlic, minced
- 1 tablespoon ginger, minced
- 1 large tomato, finely chopped
- 1 cup tomato puree
- 1 teaspoon cumin seeds
- 1 teaspoon ground coriander
- 1 teaspoon ground cumin
- 1/2 teaspoon turmeric powder
- 1/2 teaspoon red chili powder (adjust to taste)
- 1 teaspoon garam masala
- 1 teaspoon ground paprika
- Salt to taste
- 1 cup water
- Fresh cilantro for garnish

Instructions:

In a large skillet or pot, heat the vegetable oil over medium heat.
Add cumin seeds to the hot oil and let them splutter.
Add finely chopped onions and sauté until they become golden brown.
Add minced garlic and ginger to the onions and sauté for an additional 1-2 minutes until the raw smell disappears.
Add ground coriander, ground cumin, turmeric powder, red chili powder, ground paprika, and salt. Stir well to coat the onions in the spices.
Add finely chopped tomatoes and tomato puree. Cook until the tomatoes are soft and the oil starts to separate from the mixture.
Add drained and rinsed chickpeas to the pot and mix well to coat them in the spice mixture.
Pour in the water and bring the mixture to a simmer.
Cover the pot and let it cook for about 15-20 minutes on medium-low heat, allowing the flavors to meld.

Stir in garam masala and cook for an additional 5 minutes.
Adjust salt and spices to taste.
Garnish with fresh cilantro before serving.
Serve the Chana Masala hot, paired with rice, naan, or your favorite Indian bread.

Chana Masala is a delicious and satisfying vegetarian dish that's perfect for a comforting weeknight meal. The combination of chickpeas and aromatic spices makes it a flavorful and nutritious choice.

Palak Paneer (Spinach and Cottage Cheese Curry)

Ingredients:

- 2 bunches of fresh spinach, washed and blanched
- 1 cup paneer, cubed
- 2 tablespoons ghee or vegetable oil
- 1 large onion, finely chopped
- 2 tomatoes, chopped
- 1 tablespoon ginger-garlic paste
- 1 teaspoon cumin seeds
- 1 teaspoon ground coriander
- 1 teaspoon ground cumin
- 1/2 teaspoon turmeric powder
- 1/2 teaspoon red chili powder (adjust to taste)
- 1/2 teaspoon garam masala
- Salt to taste
- 1/2 cup heavy cream or yogurt (optional)
- Fresh cilantro for garnish

Instructions:

Wash the spinach thoroughly and blanch it in boiling water for 2-3 minutes. Drain and immediately transfer the spinach to ice-cold water to retain its green color. Blend the blanched spinach into a smooth puree. Set aside.
In a large skillet or pan, heat ghee or vegetable oil over medium heat.
Add cumin seeds to the hot oil and let them splutter.
Add finely chopped onions and sauté until they become golden brown.
Add ginger-garlic paste and sauté for an additional 1-2 minutes until the raw smell disappears.
Add chopped tomatoes to the pan and cook until they become soft and the oil starts to separate.
Add ground coriander, ground cumin, turmeric powder, red chili powder, and salt. Mix well and cook for another 2-3 minutes.
Pour in the spinach puree and stir well to combine with the spice mixture.
Add cubed paneer to the pan and simmer the curry for 10-15 minutes, allowing the flavors to meld.
Optional: Stir in heavy cream or yogurt for added richness.

Sprinkle garam masala over the curry and mix well.
Garnish with fresh cilantro before serving.
Serve the Palak Paneer hot, paired with rice or naan bread.

Palak Paneer is a nutritious and delicious dish that showcases the vibrant green color of spinach and the soft, creamy texture of paneer. Enjoy this classic Indian curry as a wholesome vegetarian option.

Dal Makhani

Ingredients:

- 1 cup whole black lentils (urad dal)
- 1/4 cup red kidney beans (rajma)
- 4 cups water (for soaking lentils and beans)
- 2 tablespoons ghee or unsalted butter
- 1 large onion, finely chopped
- 3 tomatoes, pureed
- 1 tablespoon ginger-garlic paste
- 1/2 teaspoon turmeric powder
- 1 teaspoon red chili powder (adjust to taste)
- 1 teaspoon ground coriander
- 1 teaspoon ground cumin
- 1 teaspoon garam masala
- Salt to taste
- 1 cup cream or full-fat milk
- Fresh cilantro for garnish

For Tempering (Tadka):

- 2 tablespoons ghee or unsalted butter
- 1 teaspoon cumin seeds
- 1/2 teaspoon red chili powder

Instructions:

Rinse black lentils and kidney beans under cold water. Soak them in 4 cups of water for at least 6 hours or overnight.

After soaking, drain the water and transfer the lentils and beans to a pressure cooker. Add fresh water and cook until they are soft and fully cooked.

In a large pan, heat ghee or butter over medium heat.

Add chopped onions and sauté until golden brown.

Add ginger-garlic paste and sauté for an additional 1-2 minutes until the raw smell disappears.

Stir in pureed tomatoes and cook until the mixture thickens, and the oil starts to separate.

Add turmeric powder, red chili powder, ground coriander, ground cumin, and garam masala. Mix well and cook for 2-3 minutes.

Add the cooked lentils and beans to the tomato mixture, along with salt. Mix well. Pour in cream or milk and simmer the dal on low heat for at least 30-40 minutes, allowing the flavors to meld.

For the tempering, heat ghee or butter in a small pan. Add cumin seeds and let them splutter. Stir in red chili powder and immediately add this tempering to the dal.

Adjust salt and spices to taste.

Garnish with fresh cilantro before serving.

Serve Dal Makhani hot, paired with rice or naan bread.

Enjoy this rich and creamy Dal Makhani, which is a perfect blend of lentils, beans, and aromatic spices. It's a comforting and satisfying dish that's sure to become a favorite.

Aloo Gobi (Potato and Cauliflower Curry)

Ingredients:

- 2 tablespoons vegetable oil
- 1 teaspoon cumin seeds
- 1 large cauliflower, cut into florets
- 2 medium-sized potatoes, peeled and cubed
- 1 large onion, finely chopped
- 2 tomatoes, chopped
- 1 tablespoon ginger-garlic paste
- 1 teaspoon turmeric powder
- 1 teaspoon ground cumin
- 1 teaspoon ground coriander
- 1/2 teaspoon red chili powder (adjust to taste)
- 1 teaspoon garam masala
- Salt to taste
- Fresh cilantro for garnish

Instructions:

Heat vegetable oil in a large pan or pot over medium heat.
Add cumin seeds to the hot oil and let them splutter.
Add finely chopped onions and sauté until they become golden brown.
Stir in ginger-garlic paste and sauté for an additional 1-2 minutes until the raw smell disappears.
Add chopped tomatoes to the pan and cook until they become soft and the oil starts to separate.
Add turmeric powder, ground cumin, ground coriander, red chili powder, and salt. Mix well and cook for another 2-3 minutes.
Add cauliflower florets and cubed potatoes to the pan. Stir to coat them in the spice mixture.
Pour in a splash of water, cover the pan, and simmer on low heat for about 20-25 minutes or until the vegetables are tender. Stir occasionally to prevent sticking.
Once the vegetables are cooked, sprinkle garam masala over the curry and mix well.
Garnish with fresh cilantro before serving.
Serve Aloo Gobi hot, paired with rice or naan bread.

This Aloo Gobi recipe results in a delicious and comforting curry with well-cooked potatoes and cauliflower, infused with the aromatic flavors of Indian spices. It's a versatile dish that can be enjoyed as a main course or a side dish.

Baingan Bharta (Roasted Eggplant Curry)

Ingredients:

- 1 large eggplant (baingan)
- 2 tablespoons vegetable oil
- 1 teaspoon cumin seeds
- 1 large onion, finely chopped
- 2 tomatoes, chopped
- 1 tablespoon ginger-garlic paste
- 1 green chili, chopped (adjust to taste)
- 1/2 teaspoon turmeric powder
- 1 teaspoon ground coriander
- 1 teaspoon ground cumin
- 1/2 teaspoon red chili powder (adjust to taste)
- 1 teaspoon garam masala
- Salt to taste
- Fresh cilantro for garnish

Instructions:

Preheat your oven broiler. Pierce the eggplant with a fork in a few places. Place the eggplant on a baking sheet and broil in the oven, turning occasionally, until the skin is charred and the flesh is soft. This may take about 15-20 minutes. Alternatively, you can roast the eggplant directly on a gas flame or on a grill. Once the eggplant is roasted, let it cool slightly. Peel off the charred skin and discard it. Mash the roasted eggplant flesh using a fork or potato masher. Set aside.
In a large pan, heat vegetable oil over medium heat.
Add cumin seeds to the hot oil and let them splutter.
Add finely chopped onions and sauté until they become golden brown.
Stir in ginger-garlic paste and chopped green chili. Sauté for an additional 1-2 minutes.
Add chopped tomatoes to the pan and cook until they become soft and the oil starts to separate.
Add turmeric powder, ground coriander, ground cumin, red chili powder, and salt. Mix well and cook for another 2-3 minutes.

Add the mashed roasted eggplant to the pan. Mix it with the spices and cook for 5-7 minutes, allowing the flavors to meld.
Sprinkle garam masala over the curry and mix well.
Garnish with fresh cilantro before serving.
Serve Baingan Bharta hot, paired with rice or naan bread.

Enjoy the smoky goodness of Baingan Bharta, a comforting and flavorful eggplant curry that's a favorite in Indian cuisine.

Fish Curry

Ingredients:

- 500g firm white fish fillets (such as cod or tilapia), cut into chunks
- 2 tablespoons vegetable oil
- 1 large onion, finely chopped
- 2 tomatoes, chopped
- 1 tablespoon ginger-garlic paste
- 1 green chili, chopped (adjust to taste)
- 1 teaspoon turmeric powder
- 1 teaspoon ground coriander
- 1 teaspoon ground cumin
- 1/2 teaspoon red chili powder (adjust to taste)
- 1 teaspoon garam masala
- Salt to taste
- 1 cup coconut milk
- Fresh cilantro for garnish

Instructions:

In a large pan, heat vegetable oil over medium heat.
Add finely chopped onions and sauté until they become golden brown.
Stir in ginger-garlic paste and chopped green chili. Sauté for an additional 1-2 minutes.
Add chopped tomatoes to the pan and cook until they become soft and the oil starts to separate.
Add turmeric powder, ground coriander, ground cumin, red chili powder, and salt. Mix well and cook for another 2-3 minutes.
Place the fish fillets in the pan and coat them with the spice mixture.
Pour in coconut milk and gently simmer the curry for 10-15 minutes or until the fish is cooked through. Be careful not to overcook the fish.
Sprinkle garam masala over the curry and mix well.
Garnish with fresh cilantro before serving.
Serve the Fish Curry hot, paired with rice or naan bread.

Feel free to adjust the spices and ingredients based on your taste preferences. This Fish Curry recipe provides a delicious and aromatic curry with tender fish chunks in a flavorful sauce.

Goan Prawn Curry

Ingredients:

- 500g large prawns, peeled and deveined
- 2 tablespoons vegetable oil
- 1 large onion, finely chopped
- 2 tomatoes, chopped
- 1 tablespoon ginger-garlic paste
- 2 green chilies, chopped (adjust to taste)
- 1 teaspoon turmeric powder
- 1 teaspoon ground coriander
- 1 teaspoon ground cumin
- 1/2 teaspoon red chili powder (adjust to taste)
- 1 teaspoon tamarind paste
- Salt to taste
- 1 cup thick coconut milk
- Fresh cilantro for garnish

For the Spice Paste:

- 1 cup grated coconut
- 1 teaspoon mustard seeds
- 1 teaspoon cumin seeds
- 6-8 dried red chilies (adjust to taste)
- 4-5 peppercorns
- 4-5 cloves
- 1-inch cinnamon stick

Instructions:

In a blender, combine all the ingredients for the spice paste and grind into a smooth paste by adding a little water if needed.
Heat vegetable oil in a large pan over medium heat.
Add finely chopped onions and sauté until they become golden brown.
Stir in ginger-garlic paste and chopped green chilies. Sauté for an additional 1-2 minutes.

Add chopped tomatoes to the pan and cook until they become soft and the oil starts to separate.

Add turmeric powder, ground coriander, ground cumin, red chili powder, tamarind paste, and salt. Mix well and cook for another 2-3 minutes.

Add the ground spice paste to the pan and cook for 5-7 minutes, allowing the flavors to meld.

Place the prawns in the pan and coat them with the spice mixture.

Pour in thick coconut milk and gently simmer the curry for 10-15 minutes or until the prawns are cooked through.

Adjust salt and spice levels to taste.

Garnish with fresh cilantro before serving.

Serve Goan Prawn Curry hot, paired with rice or crusty bread.

Enjoy the rich and aromatic flavors of this Goan Prawn Curry, a delightful coastal dish that captures the essence of Goan cuisine.

Rajma Masala (Kidney Bean Curry)

Ingredients:

- 1 cup dried kidney beans (rajma)
- 3 cups water (for soaking)
- 2 tablespoons vegetable oil
- 1 large onion, finely chopped
- 2 tomatoes, chopped
- 1 tablespoon ginger-garlic paste
- 2 green chilies, chopped (adjust to taste)
- 1 teaspoon cumin seeds
- 1 teaspoon ground coriander
- 1 teaspoon ground cumin
- 1/2 teaspoon turmeric powder
- 1 teaspoon red chili powder (adjust to taste)
- 1 teaspoon garam masala
- Salt to taste
- Fresh cilantro for garnish

Instructions:

Rinse the kidney beans under cold water and soak them in 3 cups of water for at least 6 hours or overnight.
After soaking, drain the water and transfer the kidney beans to a pressure cooker.
Add fresh water and cook until they are soft and fully cooked.
In a large pan, heat vegetable oil over medium heat.
Add cumin seeds to the hot oil and let them splutter.
Add finely chopped onions and sauté until they become golden brown.
Stir in ginger-garlic paste and chopped green chilies. Sauté for an additional 1-2 minutes.
Add chopped tomatoes to the pan and cook until they become soft and the oil starts to separate.
Add ground coriander, ground cumin, turmeric powder, red chili powder, and salt. Mix well and cook for another 2-3 minutes.
Add the cooked kidney beans to the pan. Mix them with the spice mixture.
Pour in water if needed and let the curry simmer on low heat for at least 15-20 minutes, allowing the flavors to meld.

Sprinkle garam masala over the curry and mix well.
Garnish with fresh cilantro before serving.
Serve Rajma Masala hot, paired with rice or naan bread.

Enjoy the wholesome and hearty Rajma Masala, a comforting vegetarian curry that's perfect for a satisfying meal.

Malai Kofta (Vegetable Dumplings in Creamy Tomato Sauce)

Ingredients:

For the Koftas (Dumplings):

- 2 cups mixed vegetables (carrots, peas, beans), finely chopped or grated
- 2 large potatoes, boiled and mashed
- 1/2 cup paneer (Indian cottage cheese), grated
- 1/4 cup bread crumbs
- 2 tablespoons cornflour
- 1 teaspoon ginger-garlic paste
- 1 teaspoon garam masala
- Salt to taste
- Oil for deep frying

For the Sauce:

- 2 tablespoons ghee or vegetable oil
- 1 large onion, finely chopped
- 2 tomatoes, pureed
- 1 tablespoon ginger-garlic paste
- 1/2 cup cashew nuts, soaked in warm water
- 1/4 cup fresh cream
- 1 teaspoon ground coriander
- 1 teaspoon ground cumin
- 1/2 teaspoon turmeric powder
- 1 teaspoon red chili powder (adjust to taste)
- 1 teaspoon garam masala
- Salt to taste
- 1 cup water
- Fresh cilantro for garnish

Instructions:

For the Koftas:

In a large bowl, combine the chopped or grated mixed vegetables, mashed potatoes, grated paneer, bread crumbs, cornflour, ginger-garlic paste, garam masala, and salt. Mix well to form a dough.

Divide the dough into small portions and shape them into round or oval dumplings.

Heat oil in a deep pan for frying. Once the oil is hot, deep-fry the koftas until they are golden brown and cooked through. Drain on paper towels and set aside.

For the Sauce:

In a blender, combine soaked cashew nuts with a little water and blend into a smooth paste.

In a large pan, heat ghee or vegetable oil over medium heat.

Add finely chopped onions and sauté until they become golden brown.

Stir in ginger-garlic paste and sauté for an additional 1-2 minutes.

Add pureed tomatoes to the pan and cook until the mixture thickens and the oil starts to separate.

Add ground coriander, ground cumin, turmeric powder, red chili powder, garam masala, and salt. Mix well and cook for another 2-3 minutes.

Pour in the cashew nut paste and fresh cream. Stir to combine.

Add water to achieve the desired consistency for the sauce. Simmer for 5-7 minutes.

Gently place the fried koftas into the sauce and let them simmer for an additional 5 minutes.

Garnish with fresh cilantro before serving.

Serve Malai Kofta hot, paired with rice or naan bread.

Indulge in the luxurious and creamy Malai Kofta, where the soft vegetable dumplings are bathed in a rich and flavorful tomato-based sauce. This dish is a delightful treat for special occasions or when you're craving something decadent.

Kadai Chicken

Ingredients:

- 500g boneless chicken, cut into cubes
- 2 tablespoons vegetable oil
- 1 large onion, thinly sliced
- 2 tomatoes, chopped
- 1 tablespoon ginger-garlic paste
- 2 green chilies, slit
- 1 bell pepper (capsicum), thinly sliced
- 1 teaspoon cumin seeds
- 1 teaspoon coriander seeds, crushed
- 1 teaspoon fennel seeds
- 1 teaspoon red chili powder (adjust to taste)
- 1/2 teaspoon turmeric powder
- 1 teaspoon garam masala
- Salt to taste
- Fresh cilantro for garnish

Instructions:

Heat vegetable oil in a kadai or wok over medium heat.
Add cumin seeds, crushed coriander seeds, and fennel seeds. Sauté for a minute until they release their aroma.
Add thinly sliced onions to the pan and sauté until they become golden brown.
Stir in ginger-garlic paste and green chilies. Sauté for an additional 1-2 minutes until the raw smell disappears.
Add chopped tomatoes to the pan and cook until they become soft and the oil starts to separate.
Add red chili powder, turmeric powder, and salt. Mix well and cook for another 2-3 minutes.
Place the chicken cubes in the pan and coat them with the spice mixture.
Cook the chicken until it is browned on all sides and almost cooked through.
Add thinly sliced bell pepper (capsicum) to the pan and sauté for 3-4 minutes until it is slightly tender.
Sprinkle garam masala over the chicken and mix well.
Garnish with fresh cilantro before serving.

Serve Kadai Chicken hot, paired with rice or naan bread.

Enjoy the robust and aromatic flavors of Kadai Chicken, a delightful dish that showcases the distinctive taste of spices and the unique cooking method in a kadai.

Bhindi Masala (Okra Curry)

Ingredients:

- 500g fresh okra (bhindi), washed, dried, and sliced
- 2 tablespoons vegetable oil
- 1 teaspoon cumin seeds
- 1 large onion, finely chopped
- 2 tomatoes, chopped
- 1 tablespoon ginger-garlic paste
- 2 green chilies, chopped
- 1 teaspoon ground coriander
- 1 teaspoon ground cumin
- 1/2 teaspoon turmeric powder
- 1/2 teaspoon red chili powder (adjust to taste)
- 1 teaspoon garam masala
- Salt to taste
- Fresh cilantro for garnish

Instructions:

Heat vegetable oil in a pan over medium heat.
Add cumin seeds to the hot oil and let them splutter.
Add finely chopped onions and sauté until they become golden brown.
Stir in ginger-garlic paste and chopped green chilies. Sauté for an additional 1-2 minutes until the raw smell disappears.
Add chopped tomatoes to the pan and cook until they become soft and the oil starts to separate.
Add ground coriander, ground cumin, turmeric powder, red chili powder, and salt. Mix well and cook for another 2-3 minutes.
Add sliced okra to the pan. Mix them with the spice mixture.
Cook the okra on medium heat, stirring occasionally, until it is tender and cooked through. This may take about 10-12 minutes.
Sprinkle garam masala over the curry and mix well.
Garnish with fresh cilantro before serving.
Serve Bhindi Masala hot, paired with rice or naan bread.

Enjoy the delicious and comforting Bhindi Masala, where the vibrant okra is infused with aromatic spices to create a flavorful curry. This dish is a wonderful addition to any Indian meal.

Matar Paneer (Peas and Cottage Cheese Curry)

Ingredients:

- 200g paneer, cut into cubes
- 1 cup green peas (fresh or frozen)
- 2 tablespoons vegetable oil
- 1 teaspoon cumin seeds
- 1 large onion, finely chopped
- 2 tomatoes, pureed
- 1 tablespoon ginger-garlic paste
- 1 green chili, chopped
- 1 teaspoon ground coriander
- 1 teaspoon ground cumin
- 1/2 teaspoon turmeric powder
- 1 teaspoon red chili powder (adjust to taste)
- 1 teaspoon garam masala
- Salt to taste
- 1/2 cup milk or cream
- Fresh cilantro for garnish

Instructions:

Heat vegetable oil in a pan over medium heat.
Add cumin seeds to the hot oil and let them splutter.
Add finely chopped onions and sauté until they become golden brown.
Stir in ginger-garlic paste and chopped green chili. Sauté for an additional 1-2 minutes until the raw smell disappears.
Add pureed tomatoes to the pan and cook until the mixture thickens and the oil starts to separate.
Add ground coriander, ground cumin, turmeric powder, red chili powder, and salt. Mix well and cook for another 2-3 minutes.
Add paneer cubes and green peas to the pan. Mix them with the spice mixture.
Pour in milk or cream and let the curry simmer for 10-15 minutes on low heat, allowing the flavors to meld.
Sprinkle garam masala over the curry and mix well.
Garnish with fresh cilantro before serving.
Serve Matar Paneer hot, paired with rice or naan bread.

Enjoy the delightful combination of tender paneer and sweet green peas in a luscious and aromatic tomato-based sauce. Matar Paneer is a classic vegetarian dish that's perfect for a comforting and satisfying meal.

Keema Curry (Minced Meat Curry)

Ingredients:

- 500g minced meat (beef, lamb, or chicken)
- 2 tablespoons vegetable oil
- 1 large onion, finely chopped
- 2 tomatoes, chopped
- 1 tablespoon ginger-garlic paste
- 2 green chilies, chopped
- 1 teaspoon cumin seeds
- 1 teaspoon ground coriander
- 1 teaspoon ground cumin
- 1/2 teaspoon turmeric powder
- 1 teaspoon red chili powder (adjust to taste)
- 1 teaspoon garam masala
- Salt to taste
- Fresh cilantro for garnish

Instructions:

Heat vegetable oil in a pan over medium heat.
Add cumin seeds to the hot oil and let them splutter.
Add finely chopped onions and sauté until they become golden brown.
Stir in ginger-garlic paste and chopped green chilies. Sauté for an additional 1-2 minutes until the raw smell disappears.
Add chopped tomatoes to the pan and cook until they become soft and the oil starts to separate.
Add ground coriander, ground cumin, turmeric powder, red chili powder, and salt. Mix well and cook for another 2-3 minutes.
Add minced meat to the pan. Break up the meat and mix it with the spice mixture. Cook the meat until it is browned and cooked through.
Sprinkle garam masala over the keema and mix well.
Garnish with fresh cilantro before serving.
Serve Keema Curry hot, paired with rice or naan bread.

Enjoy the rich and aromatic flavors of Keema Curry, a satisfying and comforting dish that's perfect for a hearty meal.

Dhansak (Parsi Lentil and Meat Curry)

Ingredients:

For the Dhansak Masala (Spice Mix):

- 1 tablespoon coriander seeds
- 1 teaspoon cumin seeds
- 1 teaspoon fenugreek seeds
- 1 teaspoon mustard seeds
- 1 teaspoon black peppercorns
- 1 teaspoon turmeric powder
- 1 teaspoon red chili powder

For the Curry:

- 1 cup mixed lentils (tuvar dal, masoor dal, and moong dal), washed and soaked
- 500g meat (mutton or chicken), cut into cubes
- 2 tablespoons vegetable oil
- 2 large onions, finely chopped
- 2 tomatoes, chopped
- 1 tablespoon ginger-garlic paste
- 2 tablespoons Dhansak masala (from above)
- 1/2 cup chopped vegetables (carrots, pumpkin, eggplant)
- Salt to taste
- Tamarind pulp (from a small lemon-sized tamarind soaked in water)
- 1/4 cup chopped fresh coriander for garnish

Instructions:

Prepare the Dhansak Masala:
- Dry roast coriander seeds, cumin seeds, fenugreek seeds, mustard seeds, and black peppercorns in a pan until fragrant.
- Grind the roasted spices along with turmeric powder and red chili powder to make the Dhansak masala.

Cook the Lentils:
- In a pressure cooker, cook the mixed lentils with water until soft and mushy.

Cook the Meat:

- In a separate pot, heat vegetable oil over medium heat.
- Add finely chopped onions and sauté until golden brown.
- Stir in ginger-garlic paste and sauté for an additional 1-2 minutes.
- Add chopped tomatoes to the pot and cook until they become soft and the oil starts to separate.
- Add the meat cubes to the pot and brown them.
- Mix in the Dhansak masala and cook for a couple of minutes.

Combine Lentils and Meat:
- Add the cooked lentils to the pot with the meat.
- Add chopped vegetables and salt to taste.
- Stir well, cover, and simmer until the meat and vegetables are tender.

Add Tamarind Pulp:
- Add tamarind pulp to the curry, adjusting the quantity based on your taste preferences. It should have a balance of sweet, sour, and spicy flavors.

Finish Cooking:
- Continue to simmer the Dhansak until the meat, lentils, and vegetables are fully cooked and the curry reaches the desired consistency.

Garnish and Serve:
- Garnish with chopped fresh coriander before serving.

Serve Dhansak:
- Serve Dhansak hot with steamed rice or traditional Parsi brown rice.

Dhansak is a complex and delicious dish that requires a bit of preparation but is well worth the effort. Enjoy the unique and delightful flavors of this Parsi lentil and meat curry.

Chicken Korma

Ingredients:

- 500g boneless chicken, cut into cubes
- 1/2 cup plain yogurt
- 1/2 cup cashews, soaked in warm water
- 2 tablespoons vegetable oil
- 1 large onion, finely sliced
- 2 tomatoes, pureed
- 1 tablespoon ginger-garlic paste
- 1/2 cup coconut milk
- 1/2 cup heavy cream
- 1 teaspoon ground coriander
- 1 teaspoon ground cumin
- 1/2 teaspoon turmeric powder
- 1 teaspoon red chili powder (adjust to taste)
- 1 teaspoon garam masala
- Salt to taste
- Fresh cilantro for garnish

Instructions:

Marinate the Chicken:
- In a bowl, mix chicken cubes with yogurt, ground coriander, ground cumin, turmeric powder, red chili powder, and salt. Allow it to marinate for at least 30 minutes.

Prepare the Cashew Paste:
- In a blender, blend soaked cashews with a little water to form a smooth paste.

Cook the Chicken:
- In a large pan, heat vegetable oil over medium heat.
- Add finely sliced onions and sauté until they become golden brown.
- Stir in ginger-garlic paste and sauté for an additional 1-2 minutes.
- Add pureed tomatoes to the pan and cook until the mixture thickens and the oil starts to separate.
- Add marinated chicken to the pan. Cook until the chicken is browned on all sides.

Add Cashew Paste and Coconut Milk:

- Pour in the cashew paste and coconut milk. Mix well with the chicken.
- Cover the pan and let the chicken simmer until it is cooked through.

Add Heavy Cream and Garam Masala:
- Pour in heavy cream and sprinkle garam masala over the chicken. Stir to combine.
- Allow the curry to simmer for an additional 5-7 minutes, letting the flavors meld.

Adjust Seasoning and Garnish:
- Adjust salt and spice levels according to taste.
- Garnish the Chicken Korma with fresh cilantro before serving.

Serve Chicken Korma:
- Serve the Chicken Korma hot, paired with rice, naan, or roti.

Enjoy the rich and indulgent flavors of Chicken Korma, a classic Indian dish that's perfect for a special meal or when you're craving something creamy and delicious.

Vegetable Jalfrezi

Ingredients:

- 2 tablespoons vegetable oil
- 1 teaspoon cumin seeds
- 1 large onion, thinly sliced
- 1 bell pepper (capsicum), thinly sliced
- 1 carrot, julienned
- 1 cup cauliflower florets
- 1 cup broccoli florets
- 1 cup green beans, chopped
- 1 cup peas (fresh or frozen)
- 2 tomatoes, chopped
- 1 tablespoon ginger-garlic paste
- 1 green chili, chopped (adjust to taste)
- 1 teaspoon ground coriander
- 1 teaspoon ground cumin
- 1/2 teaspoon turmeric powder
- 1 teaspoon red chili powder (adjust to taste)
- 1 teaspoon garam masala
- Salt to taste
- Fresh cilantro for garnish

Instructions:

Prepare Vegetables:
- Wash and chop all the vegetables.

Stir-Fry Vegetables:
- Heat vegetable oil in a large pan or wok over medium heat.
- Add cumin seeds to the hot oil and let them splutter.
- Add thinly sliced onions and sauté until they become golden brown.
- Stir in ginger-garlic paste and chopped green chili. Sauté for an additional 1-2 minutes.
- Add all the chopped vegetables to the pan. Stir-fry on high heat for 5-7 minutes until they are slightly tender but still have a crunch.

Add Spices:

- Add ground coriander, ground cumin, turmeric powder, red chili powder, and salt. Mix well with the vegetables.

Add Tomatoes:
- Add chopped tomatoes to the pan. Cook until the tomatoes become soft and the oil starts to separate.

Finish with Garam Masala:
- Sprinkle garam masala over the vegetables and mix well.

Adjust Seasoning and Garnish:
- Adjust salt and spice levels according to taste.
- Garnish the Vegetable Jalfrezi with fresh cilantro before serving.

Serve Vegetable Jalfrezi:
- Serve the Vegetable Jalfrezi hot, paired with rice, naan, or roti.

Enjoy this vibrant and spicy Vegetable Jalfrezi, a delightful dish that brings out the flavors of mixed vegetables in a fragrant and aromatic sauce.

Mushroom Masala

Ingredients:

- 500g mushrooms, cleaned and sliced
- 2 tablespoons vegetable oil
- 1 teaspoon cumin seeds
- 1 large onion, finely chopped
- 2 tomatoes, pureed
- 1 tablespoon ginger-garlic paste
- 1 green chili, chopped (adjust to taste)
- 1 teaspoon ground coriander
- 1 teaspoon ground cumin
- 1/2 teaspoon turmeric powder
- 1 teaspoon red chili powder (adjust to taste)
- 1 teaspoon garam masala
- Salt to taste
- Fresh cilantro for garnish

Instructions:

Prepare the Mushrooms:
- Clean the mushrooms thoroughly and slice them.

Sauté Mushrooms:
- Heat vegetable oil in a pan over medium heat.
- Add cumin seeds to the hot oil and let them splutter.
- Add sliced mushrooms to the pan and sauté until they release their water and become golden brown. Set aside.

Cook the Masala:
- In the same pan, add more oil if needed.
- Add finely chopped onions and sauté until they become golden brown.
- Stir in ginger-garlic paste and chopped green chili. Sauté for an additional 1-2 minutes.
- Add pureed tomatoes to the pan and cook until the mixture thickens and the oil starts to separate.

Add Spices:
- Add ground coriander, ground cumin, turmeric powder, red chili powder, and salt. Mix well and cook for another 2-3 minutes.

Combine Mushrooms and Masala:
- Add the sautéed mushrooms back to the pan. Mix them with the spiced tomato mixture.

Simmer and Finish:
- Allow the Mushroom Masala to simmer for 10-15 minutes on low heat, allowing the flavors to meld.
- Sprinkle garam masala over the mushrooms and mix well.

Adjust Seasoning and Garnish:
- Adjust salt and spice levels according to taste.
- Garnish the Mushroom Masala with fresh cilantro before serving.

Serve Mushroom Masala:
- Serve the Mushroom Masala hot, paired with rice, naan, or roti.

Enjoy this delightful and aromatic Mushroom Masala, a perfect option for a vegetarian meal that's quick to prepare and full of rich flavors.

Achari Chicken (Pickled Spiced Chicken)

Ingredients:

- 500g chicken, cut into pieces
- 2 tablespoons vegetable oil
- 1 teaspoon mustard seeds
- 1 teaspoon fennel seeds
- 1 teaspoon fenugreek seeds
- 1 teaspoon cumin seeds
- 1 teaspoon nigella seeds (kalonji)
- 2 tablespoons ginger-garlic paste
- 2 green chilies, chopped
- 1 large onion, finely sliced
- 2 tomatoes, chopped
- 1 tablespoon tomato paste (optional)
- 1 teaspoon turmeric powder
- 1 teaspoon red chili powder (adjust to taste)
- 1 teaspoon ground coriander
- 1 teaspoon garam masala
- Salt to taste
- Fresh coriander for garnish

Instructions:

Prepare Pickling Spice Mix:
- In a small bowl, mix mustard seeds, fennel seeds, fenugreek seeds, cumin seeds, and nigella seeds. This will be your pickling spice mix.

Marinate the Chicken:
- Rub the chicken pieces with half of the pickling spice mix, ginger-garlic paste, chopped green chilies, and salt. Allow it to marinate for at least 30 minutes.

Sauté Onions:
- In a large pan, heat vegetable oil over medium heat.
- Add the remaining pickling spice mix to the hot oil and let it sizzle.
- Add finely sliced onions and sauté until they become golden brown.

Add Tomatoes:

- Stir in chopped tomatoes and cook until they become soft and the oil starts to separate.
- Optionally, add tomato paste for extra richness and color.

Cook the Chicken:
- Add the marinated chicken to the pan. Cook until the chicken is browned on all sides.

Spice It Up:
- Add turmeric powder, red chili powder, ground coriander, and salt. Mix well with the chicken.

Simmer and Finish:
- Lower the heat and cover the pan. Let the chicken simmer until it's cooked through and the flavors meld.
- Sprinkle garam masala over the chicken and mix well.

Garnish and Serve:
- Garnish the Achari Chicken with fresh coriander before serving.

Serve Achari Chicken:
- Serve the Achari Chicken hot, paired with rice, naan, or roti.

Enjoy the tangy and aromatic flavors of Achari Chicken, a delightful twist on traditional chicken curry that's sure to impress your taste buds.

Baingan Mirch Ka Salan (Eggplant and Chili Curry)

Ingredients:

- 1 large eggplant (baingan), cut into cubes
- 4-5 green chili peppers (mirch)
- 2 tablespoons vegetable oil
- 1 teaspoon mustard seeds
- 1 teaspoon cumin seeds
- 1 large onion, finely chopped
- 2 tomatoes, chopped
- 1 tablespoon ginger-garlic paste
- 1/2 cup roasted peanuts, ground into a paste
- 1 teaspoon turmeric powder
- 1 teaspoon red chili powder (adjust to taste)
- 1 teaspoon ground coriander
- 1 teaspoon garam masala
- Salt to taste
- Fresh coriander for garnish

Instructions:

Prepare Eggplant and Chili:
- Cut the eggplant into cubes and slit the green chili peppers.

Sauté Eggplant and Chili:
- In a large pan, heat vegetable oil over medium heat.
- Add mustard seeds and cumin seeds to the hot oil. Let them splutter.
- Add the cubed eggplant and slit green chili peppers to the pan. Sauté until they are partially cooked and slightly browned. Set them aside.

Sauté Onions and Tomatoes:
- In the same pan, add more oil if needed.
- Add finely chopped onions and sauté until they become golden brown.
- Stir in ginger-garlic paste and sauté for an additional 1-2 minutes.
- Add chopped tomatoes to the pan and cook until they become soft and the oil starts to separate.

Add Ground Peanuts:
- Add the ground peanut paste to the pan. Mix well with the onion-tomato mixture.

Add Spices:
- Add turmeric powder, red chili powder, ground coriander, and salt. Mix well.

Combine Eggplant and Chili:
- Add the sautéed eggplant and chili peppers back to the pan. Mix them with the spiced peanut mixture.

Simmer and Finish:
- Lower the heat and cover the pan. Let the curry simmer until the eggplant and chili are fully cooked and the flavors meld.
- Sprinkle garam masala over the curry and mix well.

Garnish and Serve:
- Garnish Baingan Mirch Ka Salan with fresh coriander before serving.

Serve Baingan Mirch Ka Salan:
- Serve the Baingan Mirch Ka Salan hot, paired with rice or any Indian bread of your choice.

Enjoy the unique and flavorful combination of eggplant and chili in this tangy and spicy peanut-based curry!

Methi Chicken (Fenugreek Chicken Curry)

Ingredients:

- 500g chicken, cut into pieces
- 2 cups fresh fenugreek leaves (methi), cleaned and chopped
- 2 tablespoons vegetable oil
- 1 teaspoon cumin seeds
- 1 large onion, finely chopped
- 2 tomatoes, chopped
- 1 tablespoon ginger-garlic paste
- 1 green chili, chopped
- 1 teaspoon ground coriander
- 1 teaspoon ground cumin
- 1/2 teaspoon turmeric powder
- 1 teaspoon red chili powder (adjust to taste)
- 1 teaspoon garam masala
- Salt to taste
- Fresh coriander for garnish

Instructions:

Prepare Fenugreek Leaves:
- Clean and chop the fresh fenugreek leaves. You can remove the leaves from the stems.

Sauté Chicken:
- In a large pan, heat vegetable oil over medium heat.
- Add cumin seeds to the hot oil and let them splutter.
- Add chicken pieces to the pan and sauté until they are browned on all sides. Set aside.

Sauté Onions:
- In the same pan, add more oil if needed.
- Add finely chopped onions and sauté until they become golden brown.

Add Aromatics:
- Stir in ginger-garlic paste and chopped green chili. Sauté for an additional 1-2 minutes until the raw smell disappears.

Add Tomatoes:

- Add chopped tomatoes to the pan and cook until they become soft and the oil starts to separate.

Add Spices:
- Add ground coriander, ground cumin, turmeric powder, red chili powder, and salt. Mix well and cook for another 2-3 minutes.

Combine Chicken and Fenugreek Leaves:
- Add the sautéed chicken back to the pan. Mix it with the spiced onion-tomato mixture.
- Add chopped fenugreek leaves to the pan and mix well.

Simmer and Finish:
- Lower the heat and cover the pan. Let the Methi Chicken simmer until the chicken is fully cooked and the flavors meld.
- Sprinkle garam masala over the curry and mix well.

Garnish and Serve:
- Garnish Methi Chicken with fresh coriander before serving.

Serve Methi Chicken:
- Serve Methi Chicken hot, paired with rice, naan, or roti.

Enjoy the aromatic and flavorful Methi Chicken, where the unique taste of fenugreek leaves enhances the overall richness of the curry.

Lauki Kofta (Bottle Gourd Dumplings in Tomato Gravy)

Ingredients:

For Lauki Kofta:

- 2 cups grated bottle gourd (lauki)
- 1/2 cup besan (gram flour)
- 1/2 teaspoon cumin powder
- 1/2 teaspoon coriander powder
- 1/2 teaspoon red chili powder
- Salt to taste
- Oil for frying

For Tomato Gravy:

- 2 tablespoons vegetable oil
- 1 teaspoon cumin seeds
- 1 large onion, finely chopped
- 2 tomatoes, pureed
- 1 tablespoon ginger-garlic paste
- 1 teaspoon cumin powder
- 1 teaspoon coriander powder
- 1/2 teaspoon turmeric powder
- 1 teaspoon red chili powder (adjust to taste)
- 1 teaspoon garam masala
- Salt to taste
- Fresh coriander for garnish

Instructions:

Prepare Lauki Kofta:

Squeeze out excess water from grated bottle gourd.
In a bowl, combine grated bottle gourd, besan, cumin powder, coriander powder, red chili powder, and salt. Mix well to form a dough.
Divide the dough into small portions and shape them into round dumplings.

Heat oil in a pan for frying. Fry the koftas until they are golden brown and cooked through. Set aside.

Prepare Tomato Gravy:

In a large pan, heat vegetable oil over medium heat.
Add cumin seeds to the hot oil and let them splutter.
Add finely chopped onions and sauté until they become golden brown.
Stir in ginger-garlic paste and sauté for an additional 1-2 minutes until the raw smell disappears.
Add pureed tomatoes to the pan and cook until the mixture thickens and the oil starts to separate.
Add cumin powder, coriander powder, turmeric powder, red chili powder, and salt. Mix well and cook for another 2-3 minutes.
Add water to the pan to achieve the desired consistency for the gravy.
Lower the heat and add garam masala. Mix well.

Combine Kofta and Gravy:

Just before serving, add the fried Lauki Kofta to the tomato gravy. Allow them to simmer for a few minutes, letting the koftas absorb the flavors of the gravy. Garnish with fresh coriander before serving.

Serve Lauki Kofta:

Serve Lauki Kofta hot, paired with rice or any Indian bread of your choice.

Enjoy the delicious and comforting Lauki Kofta, a delightful vegetarian dish that's perfect for a special meal.

Hyderabadi Biryani

Ingredients:

For Marinating Meat:

- 500g chicken or mutton, cut into pieces
- 1 cup yogurt
- 1 tablespoon ginger-garlic paste
- 1 teaspoon red chili powder
- 1/2 teaspoon turmeric powder
- 1 teaspoon garam masala
- 1 teaspoon biryani masala
- Salt to taste
- Fresh coriander and mint leaves, chopped

For Biryani Rice:

- 2 cups basmati rice, soaked for 30 minutes
- 4-5 cups water for cooking rice
- 1-2 bay leaves
- 4-5 green cardamom pods
- 4-5 cloves
- 2-inch cinnamon stick
- Salt to taste

For Biryani Layering:

- 1/2 cup fried onions (birista)
- Saffron strands soaked in warm milk
- Ghee (clarified butter) for drizzling

Instructions:

Marinating Meat:

In a large bowl, mix together yogurt, ginger-garlic paste, red chili powder, turmeric powder, garam masala, biryani masala, salt, and chopped coriander-mint leaves. Add the chicken or mutton pieces to the marinade. Coat the meat well, cover the bowl, and let it marinate for at least 2 hours or overnight in the refrigerator for better flavor.

Cooking Biryani Rice:

Bring 4-5 cups of water to a boil in a large pot.
Add soaked basmati rice to the boiling water.
Add bay leaves, green cardamom pods, cloves, cinnamon stick, and salt to the rice.
Cook the rice until it is 70-80% done. It should have a slight bite to it.
Drain the rice and set aside.

Layering and Dum Cooking:

Preheat the oven to 350°F (180°C).
In a heavy-bottomed pan or biryani pot, layer the marinated meat at the bottom.
Add a layer of partially cooked basmati rice over the meat.
Sprinkle fried onions (birista) over the rice.
Drizzle saffron-soaked milk over the rice for color.
Drizzle ghee over the top for added richness.
Cover the pan with a tight-fitting lid or seal with aluminum foil to trap the steam.
Place the biryani pot in the preheated oven and cook for about 30-40 minutes or until the meat is tender, and the rice is fully cooked.
Alternatively, you can cook it on low heat on the stovetop, placing a griddle or tawa under the biryani pot to simulate dum cooking.
Once done, let the biryani rest for a few minutes before serving.

Serve Hyderabadi Biryani:

Gently fluff the biryani with a fork, mixing the layers just before serving. Serve hot with raita, yogurt, or a side salad.

Enjoy the rich and aromatic flavors of Hyderabadi Biryani, a classic Indian dish that's perfect for special occasions.

Prawn Masala

Ingredients:

- 500g prawns, cleaned and deveined
- 2 tablespoons vegetable oil
- 1 large onion, finely chopped
- 2 tomatoes, chopped
- 1 tablespoon ginger-garlic paste
- 1 green chili, chopped
- 1 teaspoon cumin powder
- 1 teaspoon coriander powder
- 1/2 teaspoon turmeric powder
- 1 teaspoon red chili powder (adjust to taste)
- 1 teaspoon garam masala
- Salt to taste
- Fresh coriander for garnish

Instructions:

Prepare Prawns:
- Clean and devein the prawns. You can leave the tails on for presentation.

Sauté Onions:
- In a pan, heat vegetable oil over medium heat.
- Add finely chopped onions and sauté until they become golden brown.

Add Aromatics:
- Stir in ginger-garlic paste and chopped green chili. Sauté for an additional 1-2 minutes until the raw smell disappears.

Add Tomatoes:
- Add chopped tomatoes to the pan and cook until they become soft and the oil starts to separate.

Add Spices:
- Add cumin powder, coriander powder, turmeric powder, red chili powder, and salt. Mix well and cook for another 2-3 minutes until the spices are well incorporated.

Cook Prawns:
- Add the cleaned prawns to the pan. Stir well to coat the prawns with the masala mixture.

Simmer and Finish:
- Lower the heat, cover the pan, and let the prawns simmer in the masala until they are fully cooked. This usually takes about 5-7 minutes, depending on the size of the prawns.

Sprinkle Garam Masala:
- Sprinkle garam masala over the prawns and mix well.

Garnish:
- Garnish the Prawn Masala with fresh coriander before serving.

Serve Prawn Masala:
- Serve the Prawn Masala hot, paired with rice, naan, or roti.

Enjoy the delicious and spicy flavors of Prawn Masala, a quick and easy seafood dish that's perfect for a weeknight dinner or special occasions.

Paneer Butter Masala

Ingredients:

For the Paneer:

- 250g paneer, cut into cubes
- 2 tablespoons vegetable oil
- 1 teaspoon red chili powder
- Salt to taste

For the Gravy:

- 2 tablespoons butter
- 1 tablespoon vegetable oil
- 1 large onion, finely chopped
- 2 tomatoes, pureed
- 1 tablespoon ginger-garlic paste
- 1 green chili, chopped
- 1 teaspoon cumin powder
- 1 teaspoon coriander powder
- 1/2 teaspoon turmeric powder
- 1 teaspoon red chili powder (adjust to taste)
- 1 teaspoon garam masala
- 1/2 cup cashew nuts, soaked in warm water
- 1/2 cup cream
- Salt to taste
- Fresh coriander for garnish

Instructions:

Prepare the Paneer:

>Heat vegetable oil in a pan over medium heat.
>Add red chili powder and salt to the oil.
>Add paneer cubes to the pan and sauté until they are golden brown on all sides.
>Set aside.

Prepare the Gravy:

In a separate pan, heat butter and vegetable oil over medium heat.
Add finely chopped onions and sauté until they become golden brown.
Stir in ginger-garlic paste and chopped green chili. Sauté for an additional 1-2 minutes until the raw smell disappears.
Add pureed tomatoes to the pan and cook until the mixture thickens and the oil starts to separate.
Add cumin powder, coriander powder, turmeric powder, red chili powder, and salt. Mix well and cook for another 2-3 minutes.
In a blender, combine soaked cashew nuts and cream. Blend into a smooth paste.
Add the cashew-cream paste to the pan. Mix well with the tomato-onion mixture.
Add garam masala to the pan and mix well.
Add the sautéed paneer cubes to the gravy. Stir gently to coat the paneer with the masala.
Let the Paneer Butter Masala simmer for 5-7 minutes, allowing the flavors to meld.

Garnish and Serve:

Garnish Paneer Butter Masala with fresh coriander before serving.
Serve the dish hot with naan, roti, or rice.

Enjoy the creamy and indulgent flavors of Paneer Butter Masala, a classic vegetarian dish that's loved by many!

Chicken Saagwala (Chicken in Spinach Sauce)

Ingredients:

- 500g chicken, cut into pieces
- 2 tablespoons vegetable oil
- 1 large onion, finely chopped
- 2 tomatoes, chopped
- 1 tablespoon ginger-garlic paste
- 1 green chili, chopped
- 1 teaspoon cumin powder
- 1 teaspoon coriander powder
- 1/2 teaspoon turmeric powder
- 1 teaspoon red chili powder (adjust to taste)
- 1 teaspoon garam masala
- 2 cups fresh spinach leaves, washed and chopped
- 1/2 cup fresh fenugreek leaves (optional)
- Salt to taste
- 1/2 cup cream or yogurt
- Fresh coriander for garnish

Instructions:

In a pan, heat vegetable oil over medium heat.
Add finely chopped onions to the hot oil and sauté until they become golden brown.
Stir in ginger-garlic paste and chopped green chili. Sauté for an additional 1-2 minutes until the raw smell disappears.
Add chopped tomatoes to the pan and cook until they become soft and the oil starts to separate.
Add cumin powder, coriander powder, turmeric powder, red chili powder, and salt. Mix well and cook for another 2-3 minutes.
Add fresh spinach leaves and fenugreek leaves (if using) to the pan. Mix well and cook until the leaves wilt and blend with the masala.
In a blender, puree the spinach and tomato mixture into a smooth sauce.
In the same pan, add the chicken pieces. Coat them with the masala.
Pour the spinach-tomato puree over the chicken. Mix well and let it simmer for about 10-15 minutes, or until the chicken is fully cooked.

Add garam masala to the curry. Mix well.
Stir in cream or yogurt to the Chicken Saagwala. Adjust the consistency and seasoning according to your preference.
Let the curry simmer for an additional 5 minutes, allowing the flavors to meld.
Garnish Chicken Saagwala with fresh coriander before serving.
Serve the dish hot with rice, naan, or roti.

Enjoy the wholesome and flavorful Chicken Saagwala, a delightful combination of tender chicken and nutrient-rich spinach sauce.

Aloo Methi (Potato and Fenugreek Curry)

Ingredients:

- 3-4 medium-sized potatoes, peeled and diced
- 2 cups fresh fenugreek leaves (methi), washed and chopped
- 2 tablespoons vegetable oil
- 1 teaspoon cumin seeds
- 1 large onion, finely chopped
- 1 tablespoon ginger-garlic paste
- 1 green chili, chopped
- 1 teaspoon turmeric powder
- 1 teaspoon red chili powder (adjust to taste)
- 1 teaspoon coriander powder
- Salt to taste
- Fresh coriander for garnish

Instructions:

In a pan, heat vegetable oil over medium heat.
Add cumin seeds to the hot oil and let them splutter.
Add finely chopped onions to the pan and sauté until they become golden brown.
Stir in ginger-garlic paste and chopped green chili. Sauté for an additional 1-2 minutes until the raw smell disappears.
Add diced potatoes to the pan. Mix well with the onion and spice mixture.
Cook the potatoes for about 5-7 minutes until they start to brown.
Add turmeric powder, red chili powder, coriander powder, and salt. Mix well to coat the potatoes with the spices.
Add fresh fenugreek leaves to the pan. Mix well and cook until the leaves wilt and blend with the potatoes.
Cover the pan and let the Aloo Methi simmer for about 10-15 minutes, or until the potatoes are fully cooked.
Garnish the Aloo Methi with fresh coriander before serving.
Serve the dish hot with rice or any Indian bread of your choice.

Enjoy the simple and comforting flavors of Aloo Methi, a classic vegetarian dish that highlights the earthy taste of fenugreek leaves combined with the goodness of potatoes.

Sindhi Kadhi

Ingredients:

For Kadhi:

- 1 cup gram flour (besan)
- 1 cup yogurt, beaten
- 4 cups water
- 2 tablespoons vegetable oil
- 1 teaspoon mustard seeds
- 1 teaspoon cumin seeds
- 1/2 teaspoon fenugreek seeds (methi)
- 1/2 teaspoon turmeric powder
- 1 teaspoon red chili powder (adjust to taste)
- 1 tablespoon ginger-garlic paste
- Salt to taste

For Vegetables:

- 1 cup mixed vegetables (carrots, potatoes, beans, drumsticks, etc.), chopped
- 1 large onion, sliced
- 1/2 cup tamarind pulp (soaked in water and strained)
- 2 tablespoons vegetable oil

For Tadka (Tempering):

- 2 tablespoons ghee (clarified butter)
- 1 teaspoon mustard seeds
- 1 teaspoon cumin seeds
- 2-3 dried red chilies
- A pinch of asafoetida (hing)

For Garnish:

- Fresh coriander leaves, chopped

Instructions:

Prepare Kadhi:

In a bowl, mix gram flour with beaten yogurt to form a smooth paste.
Heat vegetable oil in a pan. Add mustard seeds, cumin seeds, and fenugreek seeds. Let them splutter.
Add turmeric powder, red chili powder, and ginger-garlic paste to the pan. Sauté for a minute.
Pour the gram flour and yogurt mixture into the pan. Stir continuously to avoid lumps.
Add water gradually while stirring to achieve a smooth consistency.
Cook the kadhi on medium heat, stirring constantly, until it comes to a boil.
Lower the heat and let the kadhi simmer for about 15-20 minutes, stirring occasionally.

Prepare Vegetables:

In a separate pan, heat vegetable oil.
Add sliced onions and sauté until they become golden brown.
Add the chopped mixed vegetables to the pan and cook for a few minutes.
Add tamarind pulp to the vegetables. Mix well.
Cook until the vegetables are tender and the tamarind flavor is absorbed.

Combine Kadhi and Vegetables:

Add the cooked vegetables to the simmering kadhi. Mix well.
Let the Sindhi Kadhi cook for an additional 10-15 minutes, allowing the flavors to meld.

Prepare Tadka (Tempering):

In a small pan, heat ghee.
Add mustard seeds, cumin seeds, dried red chilies, and a pinch of asafoetida.
Once the seeds splutter, pour the tadka over the Sindhi Kadhi.

Garnish and Serve:

Garnish Sindhi Kadhi with fresh coriander leaves.
Serve hot with rice or any Indian bread.

Enjoy the delightful and tangy flavors of Sindhi Kadhi, a traditional dish that brings together the goodness of vegetables and the richness of the gram flour and yogurt-based curry.

Keema Matar (Minced Meat with Peas)

Ingredients:

- 500g minced meat (chicken, lamb, or beef)
- 2 tablespoons vegetable oil
- 1 large onion, finely chopped
- 1 tablespoon ginger-garlic paste
- 2 tomatoes, chopped
- 1 teaspoon cumin powder
- 1 teaspoon coriander powder
- 1/2 teaspoon turmeric powder
- 1 teaspoon red chili powder (adjust to taste)
- 1/2 teaspoon garam masala
- 1 cup frozen peas
- Salt to taste
- Fresh coriander for garnish

Instructions:

In a pan, heat vegetable oil over medium heat.
Add finely chopped onions to the hot oil and sauté until they become golden brown.
Stir in ginger-garlic paste and sauté for an additional 1-2 minutes until the raw smell disappears.
Add chopped tomatoes to the pan and cook until they become soft and the oil starts to separate.
Add cumin powder, coriander powder, turmeric powder, red chili powder, and salt. Mix well and cook for another 2-3 minutes.
Add the minced meat to the pan. Break it apart and mix well with the masala.
Cook the minced meat until it is browned and cooked through.
Add garam masala to the pan. Mix well.
Stir in frozen peas and cook for an additional 5-7 minutes until the peas are tender.
Garnish Keema Matar with fresh coriander before serving.
Serve the dish hot with rice or any Indian bread of your choice.

Enjoy the hearty and flavorful Keema Matar, a comforting dish that pairs well with rice, naan, or roti.

Chicken Vindaloo

Ingredients:

For Marination:

- 500g chicken, cut into pieces
- 2 tablespoons vinegar
- 1 teaspoon ginger-garlic paste
- 1 teaspoon cumin powder
- 1 teaspoon coriander powder
- 1/2 teaspoon turmeric powder
- 1 teaspoon red chili powder (adjust to taste)
- Salt to taste

For Vindaloo Masala Paste:

- 2 tablespoons vegetable oil
- 1 large onion, finely chopped
- 3-4 dry red chilies, soaked in warm water
- 1 teaspoon mustard seeds
- 1 teaspoon cumin seeds
- 1 teaspoon fenugreek seeds (methi)
- 1/2 teaspoon black peppercorns
- 4-5 cloves of garlic
- 1-inch ginger, chopped
- 1 teaspoon turmeric powder
- 1 tablespoon red chili powder (adjust to taste)
- 1 teaspoon paprika (optional, for color)
- 1 teaspoon cinnamon powder
- 2-3 cloves
- 2-3 green cardamom pods
- 1 teaspoon sugar
- Salt to taste
- 2 tablespoons vinegar

For Cooking:

- 2 tablespoons vegetable oil

- 1 large onion, finely sliced
- 1 large tomato, chopped
- Fresh coriander for garnish

Instructions:

Marinate the Chicken:

In a bowl, mix the chicken pieces with vinegar, ginger-garlic paste, cumin powder, coriander powder, turmeric powder, red chili powder, and salt. Let it marinate for at least 1-2 hours or overnight for better flavor.

Prepare Vindaloo Masala Paste:

In a pan, heat 2 tablespoons of oil over medium heat.
Add chopped onions and sauté until they become golden brown.
In a blender, combine soaked red chilies, mustard seeds, cumin seeds, fenugreek seeds, black peppercorns, garlic, ginger, turmeric powder, red chili powder, paprika (if using), cinnamon powder, cloves, cardamom pods, sugar, and salt. Add sautéed onions to the blender and blend everything into a smooth paste, adding vinegar to aid in the blending process.

Cook Chicken Vindaloo:

In a pan, heat 2 tablespoons of oil over medium heat.
Add finely sliced onions and sauté until they become translucent.
Add chopped tomatoes to the pan and cook until they become soft and the oil starts to separate.
Add the marinated chicken to the pan and cook until it is browned.
Stir in the Vindaloo masala paste and mix well with the chicken.
Cook the Chicken Vindaloo for about 15-20 minutes, allowing the flavors to meld and the chicken to cook through.
Garnish with fresh coriander before serving.
Serve hot with rice or any Indian bread.

Enjoy the bold and spicy flavors of Chicken Vindaloo, a delicious and iconic dish from Indian cuisine.

Tomato Pappu (Tomato Lentil Curry)

Ingredients:

- 1 cup toor dal (split pigeon peas), rinsed
- 3 cups water
- 2 tomatoes, chopped
- 1 onion, chopped
- 2 green chilies, slit lengthwise
- 1 teaspoon mustard seeds
- 1 teaspoon cumin seeds
- 1/2 teaspoon turmeric powder
- 1 teaspoon red chili powder (adjust to taste)
- 1/2 teaspoon asafoetida (hing)
- 1 tablespoon tamarind paste
- Salt to taste
- 2 tablespoons vegetable oil
- Fresh coriander leaves for garnish

Instructions:

In a pressure cooker or a pot, add rinsed toor dal and water. Cook the dal until it becomes soft and mushy. If using a pressure cooker, cook for about 4-5 whistles. If using a pot, cook for about 30-40 minutes, stirring occasionally and adding more water if necessary.

Once the dal is cooked, mash it well using a spoon or a potato masher. Set aside.

In a separate pan, heat vegetable oil over medium heat.

Add mustard seeds to the hot oil and let them splutter.

Add cumin seeds and let them sizzle.

Add chopped onions and green chilies to the pan. Sauté until the onions become translucent.

Add chopped tomatoes to the pan and cook until they become soft and mushy.

Stir in turmeric powder, red chili powder, and asafoetida. Mix well.

Add the cooked and mashed toor dal to the pan. Mix well with the tomato-onion mixture.

Add tamarind paste and salt to the dal mixture. Mix well and let it simmer for about 5-10 minutes, allowing the flavors to meld.

If the Tomato Pappu is too thick, you can add some water to adjust the consistency.

Garnish with fresh coriander leaves before serving.
Serve hot with rice or any Indian bread of your choice.

Enjoy the comforting and flavorful Tomato Pappu, a classic South Indian dish that's perfect for a comforting meal.

Nihari

Ingredients:

For Nihari Masala:

- 2 tablespoons coriander seeds
- 1 tablespoon fennel seeds
- 1 tablespoon cumin seeds
- 1 tablespoon black peppercorns
- 1 tablespoon whole cloves
- 4-5 green cardamom pods
- 2 black cardamom pods
- 1 cinnamon stick
- 1 dried bay leaf

For Nihari:

- 1 kg beef or mutton, cut into pieces
- 4 tablespoons ghee or vegetable oil
- 2 large onions, thinly sliced
- 1 tablespoon ginger paste
- 1 tablespoon garlic paste
- 2 tablespoons Nihari masala (from above)
- 1 teaspoon turmeric powder
- 1 teaspoon red chili powder (adjust to taste)
- Salt to taste
- 4 cups water
- 2 tablespoons wheat flour (optional, for thickening)
- Fresh coriander and thinly sliced ginger for garnish

Instructions:

Prepare Nihari Masala:

In a dry pan, roast coriander seeds, fennel seeds, cumin seeds, black peppercorns, whole cloves, green cardamom pods, black cardamom pods, cinnamon stick, and dried bay leaf until they become aromatic. Be careful not to burn them.

Let the roasted spices cool and then grind them into a fine powder. This is your Nihari masala.

Cook Nihari:

In a large pot, heat ghee or vegetable oil over medium heat.

Add thinly sliced onions and cook until they become golden brown.

Add ginger paste and garlic paste to the pot. Sauté for 1-2 minutes until the raw smell disappears.

Add meat pieces to the pot and brown them on all sides.

Stir in Nihari masala, turmeric powder, red chili powder, and salt. Mix well to coat the meat with the spices.

Pour in water and bring the mixture to a boil. Once boiling, reduce the heat to low, cover the pot, and let it simmer for several hours (3-4 hours or more), until the meat is tender and the flavors have melded. You can also use a slow cooker for this step.

Optional: In a small bowl, mix wheat flour with some water to create a smooth paste. Add this paste to the pot to thicken the Nihari. Cook for an additional 30 minutes.

Garnish Nihari with fresh coriander and thinly sliced ginger.

Serve hot with naan or rice.

Enjoy the rich and aromatic flavors of homemade Nihari, a dish that's traditionally enjoyed as a special treat during breakfast or brunch.

Gatte Ki Sabzi (Gram Flour Dumplings in Yogurt Gravy)

Ingredients:

For Gatte (Gram Flour Dumplings):

- 1 cup gram flour (besan)
- 1/4 teaspoon carom seeds (ajwain)
- 1/4 teaspoon turmeric powder
- 1/2 teaspoon red chili powder
- 1/2 teaspoon coriander powder
- 1/4 teaspoon asafoetida (hing)
- Salt to taste
- Water (as needed)
- 2 tablespoons oil

For Gravy:

- 2 cups yogurt, beaten
- 2 tablespoons gram flour (besan)
- 1 tablespoon oil
- 1 teaspoon cumin seeds
- 1/2 teaspoon mustard seeds
- 1/4 teaspoon asafoetida (hing)
- 1 onion, finely chopped
- 1 tablespoon ginger-garlic paste
- 1 teaspoon coriander powder
- 1/2 teaspoon turmeric powder
- 1 teaspoon red chili powder
- 1 teaspoon garam masala
- Salt to taste
- Fresh coriander leaves for garnish

Instructions:

Prepare Gatte (Gram Flour Dumplings):

In a mixing bowl, combine gram flour, carom seeds, turmeric powder, red chili powder, coriander powder, asafoetida, salt, and oil.
Gradually add water to the mixture and knead it into a smooth and firm dough.
Divide the dough into small portions and shape them into cylindrical rolls (gatte).
In a large pot, bring water to a boil. Add the gatte and let them cook for about 15-20 minutes or until they are firm and cooked through.
Once cooked, remove the gatte from water, let them cool, and then slice them into rounds.

Prepare Gravy:

In a bowl, mix beaten yogurt and gram flour until smooth. Set aside.
In a pan, heat oil over medium heat.
Add cumin seeds, mustard seeds, and asafoetida. Let them splutter.
Add finely chopped onions and sauté until they become golden brown.
Stir in ginger-garlic paste and sauté for an additional 1-2 minutes.
Add coriander powder, turmeric powder, red chili powder, and salt. Mix well.
Pour in the yogurt and gram flour mixture. Stir continuously to avoid lumps.
Cook the gravy until it thickens and the oil starts to separate.
Add garam masala to the gravy. Mix well.

Combine Gatte and Gravy:

Gently add the sliced gatte to the gravy. Stir carefully to coat the gatte with the gravy.
Let the Gatte Ki Sabzi simmer for about 10-15 minutes, allowing the flavors to meld.

Garnish and Serve:

Garnish Gatte Ki Sabzi with fresh coriander leaves.
Serve hot with rice or any Indian bread of your choice.

Enjoy the delicious and comforting flavors of Gatte Ki Sabzi, a classic Rajasthani dish that's perfect for a hearty meal.

Chicken Chettinad

Ingredients:

For Marination:

- 500g chicken, cleaned and cut into pieces
- 1 teaspoon turmeric powder
- 1 teaspoon red chili powder
- Salt to taste
- 1 tablespoon ginger-garlic paste

For Chettinad Masala Paste:

- 1 tablespoon vegetable oil
- 1 teaspoon cumin seeds
- 1 teaspoon fennel seeds
- 1 tablespoon coriander seeds
- 1 tablespoon poppy seeds
- 4-5 dry red chilies
- 1 onion, sliced
- 1 tomato, chopped
- 5-6 cloves garlic
- 1-inch ginger, chopped
- 1/2 cup fresh coconut, grated
- 1 tablespoon tamarind paste

For Curry:

- 2 tablespoons vegetable oil
- 2 onions, finely chopped
- 1 sprig curry leaves
- 1 cinnamon stick
- 2-3 green cardamom pods
- 2-3 cloves
- 1 teaspoon mustard seeds
- 1 teaspoon fennel seeds

- Salt to taste
- Fresh coriander leaves for garnish

Instructions:

Marinate the Chicken:

In a bowl, combine chicken pieces with turmeric powder, red chili powder, salt, and ginger-garlic paste. Let it marinate for at least 30 minutes.

Prepare Chettinad Masala Paste:

In a pan, heat 1 tablespoon of oil over medium heat.
Add cumin seeds, fennel seeds, coriander seeds, poppy seeds, and dry red chilies. Roast until they become aromatic. Be careful not to burn them.
Add sliced onions, chopped tomatoes, garlic, and ginger to the pan. Sauté until the onions become translucent.
Add grated coconut to the pan and continue to sauté until everything is well-cooked.
Allow the mixture to cool and then blend it into a smooth paste along with tamarind paste.

Cook the Chicken Chettinad:

In a large pan or kadai, heat 2 tablespoons of oil over medium heat.
Add mustard seeds, fennel seeds, curry leaves, cinnamon stick, green cardamom pods, and cloves. Let them splutter.
Add finely chopped onions and sauté until they become golden brown.
Add the marinated chicken to the pan and cook until it is browned.
Stir in the Chettinad masala paste and mix well with the chicken.
Cook the Chicken Chettinad for about 15-20 minutes, allowing the chicken to cook through and absorb the flavors.
Adjust salt to taste and garnish with fresh coriander leaves before serving.
Serve hot with rice or any Indian bread of your choice.

Enjoy the bold and spicy flavors of Chicken Chettinad, a delightful South Indian dish that's sure to satisfy your taste buds.

Baingan Patiala (Eggplant in Tomato Onion Gravy)

Ingredients:

- 500g small eggplants (baby brinjals), slit into four without cutting through
- 2 tablespoons oil
- 1 teaspoon cumin seeds
- 1 onion, finely chopped
- 1 tablespoon ginger-garlic paste
- 2 tomatoes, pureed
- 1 teaspoon turmeric powder
- 1 teaspoon red chili powder (adjust to taste)
- 1 teaspoon coriander powder
- 1 teaspoon garam masala
- Salt to taste
- Fresh coriander leaves for garnish

Instructions:

Heat oil in a pan over medium heat. Add cumin seeds and let them splutter.
Add finely chopped onions to the pan and sauté until they become golden brown.
Stir in ginger-garlic paste and sauté for an additional 1-2 minutes until the raw smell disappears.
Add tomato puree to the pan and cook until the oil starts to separate from the masala.
Mix in turmeric powder, red chili powder, coriander powder, and salt. Cook the masala for another 3-4 minutes.
Slit the eggplants into four without cutting through, creating a cross shape.
Carefully stuff the eggplants with the prepared masala.
Place the stuffed eggplants in the pan with the masala, ensuring they are well-coated with the gravy.
Add a little water to the pan, cover it, and let the eggplants cook on low heat until they are tender. Stir occasionally to avoid burning.
Once the eggplants are cooked, sprinkle garam masala over them and garnish with fresh coriander leaves.
Serve hot with Indian bread (roti) or rice.

Enjoy the flavorsome Baingan Patiala, a delightful vegetarian dish that showcases the rich taste of eggplants in a savory tomato-onion gravy.

Murgh Do Pyaza (Chicken with Double Onions)

Ingredients:

- 500g chicken, cut into pieces
- 2 large onions, thinly sliced
- 2 medium-sized onions, finely chopped
- 2 tomatoes, finely chopped
- 1 tablespoon ginger-garlic paste
- 1 cup yogurt, whisked
- 2 tablespoons vegetable oil
- 1 teaspoon cumin seeds
- 2-3 green cardamom pods
- 2-3 cloves
- 1 cinnamon stick
- 1 bay leaf
- 1 teaspoon turmeric powder
- 1 teaspoon red chili powder (adjust to taste)
- 1 teaspoon coriander powder
- 1 teaspoon garam masala
- Salt to taste
- Fresh coriander leaves for garnish

Instructions:

In a pan, heat oil over medium heat. Add cumin seeds, green cardamom pods, cloves, cinnamon stick, and bay leaf. Let them splutter.
Add thinly sliced onions to the pan and sauté until they become golden brown.
Stir in ginger-garlic paste and sauté for an additional 1-2 minutes until the raw smell disappears.
Add finely chopped tomatoes to the pan and cook until they become soft and the oil starts to separate.
Mix in turmeric powder, red chili powder, coriander powder, and salt. Cook the masala for another 3-4 minutes.
Add chicken pieces to the pan and brown them on all sides.
Add chopped onions to the pan and sauté until they are translucent.
Pour whisked yogurt into the pan and mix well with the chicken and onions.
Cover the pan and let the chicken cook on low heat until it is tender. Stir occasionally to avoid burning.

Sprinkle garam masala over the Murgh Do Pyaza and garnish with fresh coriander leaves.
Serve hot with Indian bread (roti) or rice.

Enjoy the delectable Murgh Do Pyaza, a dish that brings together the richness of chicken and the sweetness of double onions in a savory curry.

Methi Malai Murg (Fenugreek Cream Chicken)

Ingredients:

- 500g chicken, cut into pieces
- 1 cup fresh fenugreek leaves (methi), chopped
- 1 cup onions, finely chopped
- 1 tablespoon ginger-garlic paste
- 2 tomatoes, pureed
- 1 cup fresh cream
- 1/2 cup milk
- 2 tablespoons ghee or vegetable oil
- 1 teaspoon cumin seeds
- 2-3 green cardamom pods
- 2-3 cloves
- 1 cinnamon stick
- 1 bay leaf
- 1 teaspoon turmeric powder
- 1 teaspoon red chili powder (adjust to taste)
- 1 teaspoon coriander powder
- 1/2 teaspoon garam masala
- Salt to taste
- Fresh coriander leaves for garnish

Instructions:

In a pan, heat ghee or vegetable oil over medium heat. Add cumin seeds, green cardamom pods, cloves, cinnamon stick, and bay leaf. Let them splutter.

Add finely chopped onions to the pan and sauté until they become golden brown.

Stir in ginger-garlic paste and sauté for an additional 1-2 minutes until the raw smell disappears.

Add pureed tomatoes to the pan and cook until they become soft and the oil starts to separate.

Mix in turmeric powder, red chili powder, coriander powder, and salt. Cook the masala for another 3-4 minutes.

Add chicken pieces to the pan and brown them on all sides.

Once the chicken is browned, add fresh fenugreek leaves (methi) to the pan. Sauté until the leaves wilt.

Pour in fresh cream and milk to the pan. Mix well with the chicken and fenugreek leaves.

Cover the pan and let the Methi Malai Murg simmer on low heat until the chicken is tender and the flavors meld.

Sprinkle garam masala over the dish and garnish with fresh coriander leaves.

Serve hot with Indian bread (roti) or rice.

Enjoy the rich and creamy Methi Malai Murg, a dish that combines the earthy flavors of fenugreek with the luxuriousness of cream for a delightful culinary experience.

Khumb Matar (Mushroom and Peas Curry)

Ingredients:

- 250g mushrooms, cleaned and sliced
- 1 cup green peas (fresh or frozen)
- 2 tablespoons vegetable oil
- 1 large onion, finely chopped
- 2 tomatoes, pureed
- 1 tablespoon ginger-garlic paste
- 1 teaspoon cumin seeds
- 1 teaspoon coriander powder
- 1/2 teaspoon turmeric powder
- 1 teaspoon red chili powder (adjust to taste)
- 1 teaspoon garam masala
- Salt to taste
- Fresh coriander leaves for garnish

Instructions:

In a pan, heat vegetable oil over medium heat. Add cumin seeds and let them splutter.
Add finely chopped onions to the pan and sauté until they become golden brown.
Stir in ginger-garlic paste and sauté for an additional 1-2 minutes until the raw smell disappears.
Add pureed tomatoes to the pan and cook until they become soft and the oil starts to separate.
Mix in coriander powder, turmeric powder, red chili powder, and salt. Cook the masala for another 3-4 minutes.
Add sliced mushrooms to the pan and sauté until they release their moisture and become tender.
Add green peas to the pan and mix well with the masala.
Pour in water to achieve the desired consistency of the curry. Cover the pan and let it simmer until the mushrooms and peas are fully cooked.
Sprinkle garam masala over the Khumb Matar and garnish with fresh coriander leaves.
Serve hot with Indian bread (roti) or rice.

Enjoy the delicious and wholesome Khumb Matar, a vegetarian curry that pairs the earthiness of mushrooms with the sweetness of peas in a flavorful gravy.

Chicken Kolhapuri

Ingredients:

For Marination:

- 500g chicken, cut into pieces
- 1 teaspoon turmeric powder
- 1 teaspoon red chili powder
- Salt to taste
- 1 tablespoon vegetable oil

For Kolhapuri Masala:

- 1 tablespoon vegetable oil
- 1 onion, sliced
- 1 cup grated coconut (fresh or desiccated)
- 2 tablespoons sesame seeds
- 2 tablespoons poppy seeds
- 5-6 dry red chilies (adjust to taste)
- 1 tablespoon coriander seeds
- 1 tablespoon cumin seeds
- 1 tablespoon fennel seeds
- 4-5 green cardamom pods
- 4-5 cloves
- 2-inch cinnamon stick
- 1 black cardamom pod
- 1 bay leaf

For Curry:

- 2 tablespoons vegetable oil
- 1 onion, finely chopped
- 1 tablespoon ginger-garlic paste
- 2 tomatoes, pureed
- Salt to taste
- Fresh coriander leaves for garnish

Instructions:

Marinate the Chicken:

In a bowl, mix chicken pieces with turmeric powder, red chili powder, salt, and 1 tablespoon of vegetable oil. Let it marinate for at least 30 minutes.

Prepare Kolhapuri Masala:

In a pan, heat 1 tablespoon of oil over medium heat.
Add sliced onions to the pan and sauté until they become golden brown.
Add grated coconut, sesame seeds, poppy seeds, dry red chilies, coriander seeds, cumin seeds, fennel seeds, green cardamom pods, cloves, cinnamon stick, black cardamom pod, and bay leaf to the pan. Roast the spices until they release their aroma. Be careful not to burn them.
Allow the mixture to cool and then grind it into a fine paste using a blender or food processor. You can add a little water to make a smooth paste.

Cook the Chicken Kolhapuri:

In a pan, heat 2 tablespoons of oil over medium heat.
Add finely chopped onions to the pan and sauté until they become translucent.
Stir in ginger-garlic paste and sauté for an additional 1-2 minutes until the raw smell disappears.
Add pureed tomatoes to the pan and cook until they become soft and the oil starts to separate.
Add the marinated chicken to the pan and brown it on all sides.
Mix in the prepared Kolhapuri masala paste and salt. Stir well to coat the chicken with the masala.
Cover the pan and let the Chicken Kolhapuri cook on low heat until the chicken is tender and the flavors meld. Stir occasionally to prevent burning.
Garnish with fresh coriander leaves before serving.
Serve hot with Indian bread (roti) or rice.

Enjoy the bold and spicy flavors of Chicken Kolhapuri, a dish that showcases the rich and aromatic taste of Kolhapuri spices.

Palak Kofta Curry (Spinach Dumplings in Tomato Gravy)

Ingredients:

For Spinach Koftas:

- 2 cups spinach, finely chopped
- 1 cup paneer (Indian cottage cheese), grated
- 1/2 cup besan (gram flour)
- 1/2 teaspoon cumin powder
- 1/2 teaspoon garam masala
- 1/2 teaspoon red chili powder
- Salt to taste
- Oil for deep frying

For Gravy:

- 2 tablespoons vegetable oil
- 1 large onion, finely chopped
- 2 tomatoes, pureed
- 1 tablespoon ginger-garlic paste
- 1 teaspoon cumin seeds
- 1 teaspoon coriander powder
- 1/2 teaspoon turmeric powder
- 1/2 teaspoon red chili powder (adjust to taste)
- 1/2 teaspoon garam masala
- Salt to taste
- 1/2 cup cream or cashew paste (optional)
- Fresh coriander leaves for garnish

Instructions:

Prepare Spinach Koftas:

In a mixing bowl, combine finely chopped spinach, grated paneer, besan, cumin powder, garam masala, red chili powder, and salt.
Mix the ingredients well to form a dough-like consistency.

Shape the mixture into small, round koftas.

Heat oil in a deep frying pan. Once the oil is hot, deep fry the koftas until they are golden brown and crispy. Remove them and place on paper towels to absorb excess oil.

Prepare Gravy:

In a separate pan, heat vegetable oil over medium heat. Add cumin seeds and let them splutter.

Add finely chopped onions to the pan and sauté until they become golden brown.

Stir in ginger-garlic paste and sauté for an additional 1-2 minutes until the raw smell disappears.

Add pureed tomatoes to the pan and cook until they become soft and the oil starts to separate.

Mix in coriander powder, turmeric powder, red chili powder, garam masala, and salt. Cook the masala for another 3-4 minutes.

Add cream or cashew paste (if using) to the pan. Mix well with the masala.

Allow the gravy to simmer for a few minutes until it thickens.

Combine Koftas and Gravy:

Just before serving, gently add the fried spinach koftas to the simmering gravy. Be careful not to break them.

Let the Palak Kofta Curry cook for an additional 5-7 minutes, allowing the koftas to absorb the flavors of the gravy.

Garnish and Serve:

Garnish Palak Kofta Curry with fresh coriander leaves.

Serve hot with Indian bread (roti) or rice.

Enjoy the delightful Palak Kofta Curry, a dish that brings together the goodness of spinach dumplings with a luscious tomato-based gravy.

Dal Tadka

Ingredients:

- 1 cup yellow lentils (toor dal)
- 1/2 teaspoon turmeric powder
- 1 teaspoon salt (or to taste)
- 4 cups water
- 2 tablespoons ghee (clarified butter) or oil
- 1 teaspoon cumin seeds
- 1 teaspoon mustard seeds
- 2-3 dry red chilies
- 1 onion, finely chopped
- 2 tomatoes, chopped
- 1 tablespoon ginger-garlic paste
- 1 teaspoon coriander powder
- 1/2 teaspoon red chili powder (adjust to taste)
- 1/2 teaspoon garam masala
- Fresh coriander leaves for garnish

Instructions:

Cooking Lentils:

Rinse the yellow lentils thoroughly under running water.
In a pressure cooker, combine the rinsed lentils, turmeric powder, salt, and water.
Pressure cook the lentils for 3-4 whistles or until they are soft and mushy.
Once the pressure is released, mash the lentils using a spoon or a dal masher.
Set aside.

Tempering (Tadka):

In a separate pan, heat ghee or oil over medium heat.
Add cumin seeds and mustard seeds. Let them splutter.
Add dry red chilies to the pan and sauté for a few seconds.
Add finely chopped onions and sauté until they become golden brown.

Stir in ginger-garlic paste and sauté for an additional 1-2 minutes until the raw smell disappears.

Add chopped tomatoes to the pan and cook until they become soft.

Mix in coriander powder, red chili powder, and garam masala. Sauté the spices for 2-3 minutes.

Combining Lentils and Tempering:

Add the mashed lentils to the tempering mixture. Mix well to combine.

Adjust the consistency of the dal by adding water if needed. Bring it to a gentle boil.

Check and adjust the salt and spice levels according to your taste.

Let the Dal Tadka simmer for a few minutes, allowing the flavors to meld.

Garnish and Serve:

Garnish Dal Tadka with fresh coriander leaves.

Serve hot with steamed rice or Indian bread (roti, naan).

Enjoy the warm and comforting flavors of Dal Tadka, a classic Indian lentil dish that's simple to prepare yet incredibly delicious.

Shahi Paneer

Ingredients:

For Paneer Marinade:

- 250g paneer, cut into cubes
- 1/2 cup thick yogurt
- 1 teaspoon ginger-garlic paste
- 1/2 teaspoon turmeric powder
- 1/2 teaspoon red chili powder
- Salt to taste

For Shahi Gravy:

- 2 tablespoons ghee or vegetable oil
- 1 onion, finely chopped
- 2 tomatoes, pureed
- 1/2 cup cashews, soaked in warm water
- 1/2 cup fresh cream
- 1 teaspoon ginger-garlic paste
- 1 teaspoon cumin seeds
- 1/2 teaspoon turmeric powder
- 1/2 teaspoon red chili powder (adjust to taste)
- 1 teaspoon coriander powder
- 1/2 teaspoon garam masala
- Salt to taste
- 1/2 cup milk (optional, for adjusting consistency)
- Fresh coriander leaves for garnish

Instructions:

Marinate Paneer:

In a bowl, combine yogurt, ginger-garlic paste, turmeric powder, red chili powder, and salt.

Add paneer cubes to the marinade and coat them well. Let it marinate for at least 30 minutes.

Prepare Shahi Gravy:

In a blender, make a smooth paste by blending soaked cashews and a little water.
In a pan, heat ghee or vegetable oil over medium heat. Add cumin seeds and let them splutter.
Add finely chopped onions to the pan and sauté until they become golden brown.
Stir in ginger-garlic paste and sauté for an additional 1-2 minutes until the raw smell disappears.
Add pureed tomatoes to the pan and cook until they become soft and the oil starts to separate.
Mix in turmeric powder, red chili powder, coriander powder, and salt. Cook the masala for another 3-4 minutes.
Add the cashew paste to the pan and cook for a few more minutes, allowing it to thicken.
Pour in fresh cream and garam masala. Mix well with the masala.
If the gravy is too thick, you can adjust the consistency by adding milk.

Cook Paneer in Shahi Gravy:

Add the marinated paneer cubes to the Shahi gravy. Gently mix to coat the paneer with the creamy sauce.
Let the Shahi Paneer simmer on low heat for 5-7 minutes, allowing the flavors to meld.

Garnish and Serve:

Garnish Shahi Paneer with fresh coriander leaves.
Serve hot with Indian bread (naan, roti) or rice.

Enjoy the luxurious and flavorful Shahi Paneer, a dish fit for royalty that brings together the richness of paneer and the creaminess of the Shahi gravy.

Malabar Fish Curry

Ingredients:

- 500g fish fillets (such as kingfish, pomfret, or any firm white fish)
- 1 cup thick coconut milk
- 1/2 cup thin coconut milk
- 2 tablespoons vegetable oil
- 1 teaspoon mustard seeds
- 1 sprig curry leaves
- 2 onions, thinly sliced
- 2 tomatoes, chopped
- 1 tablespoon ginger-garlic paste
- 2 green chilies, slit
- 1 teaspoon turmeric powder
- 2 teaspoons red chili powder (adjust to taste)
- 1 tablespoon coriander powder
- 1/2 teaspoon fenugreek seeds
- Salt to taste
- Fresh coriander leaves for garnish

Instructions:

Clean and cut the fish into medium-sized pieces. Rub the fish pieces with salt and turmeric powder. Set aside for a few minutes.
In a pan, heat vegetable oil over medium heat. Add mustard seeds and let them splutter.
Add fenugreek seeds and curry leaves to the pan. Sauté for a few seconds.
Add thinly sliced onions to the pan and sauté until they become golden brown.
Stir in ginger-garlic paste and sauté for an additional 1-2 minutes until the raw smell disappears.
Add chopped tomatoes to the pan and cook until they become soft.
Mix in turmeric powder, red chili powder, and coriander powder. Sauté the spices for 2-3 minutes.
Pour in thin coconut milk to the pan. Bring it to a gentle boil.
Add the fish pieces to the pan and let them cook in the thin coconut milk for about 5-7 minutes or until they are almost done.
Pour in thick coconut milk and add slit green chilies. Adjust salt according to taste. Simmer for an additional 5-7 minutes.

Garnish the Malabar Fish Curry with fresh coriander leaves.
Serve hot with steamed rice or Malabar paratha.

Enjoy the authentic flavors of Malabar Fish Curry, a delicious and aromatic dish that showcases the rich culinary heritage of Kerala.

Punjabi Kadhi Pakora

Ingredients:

For Kadhi:

- 1 cup yogurt (curd), whisked
- 1/4 cup besan (gram flour)
- 2 tablespoons vegetable oil
- 1 teaspoon mustard seeds
- 1 teaspoon cumin seeds
- 1/2 teaspoon fenugreek seeds (methi)
- 1/2 teaspoon turmeric powder
- 1 teaspoon red chili powder
- 2 green chilies, chopped
- 1 tablespoon ginger-garlic paste
- 10-12 curry leaves
- Salt to taste
- 4 cups water

For Pakoras:

- 1 cup besan (gram flour)
- 1/2 teaspoon carom seeds (ajwain)
- 1/2 teaspoon turmeric powder
- 1/2 teaspoon red chili powder
- Salt to taste
- Water (as needed to make a thick batter)
- Vegetable oil for deep frying

For Tempering:

- 2 tablespoons ghee or vegetable oil
- 1 teaspoon mustard seeds
- 1 teaspoon cumin seeds
- 2 dried red chilies
- 1/2 teaspoon asafoetida (hing)

Instructions:

Prepare Kadhi:

- In a bowl, whisk yogurt and besan together to form a smooth paste.
- In a large pot, heat vegetable oil over medium heat. Add mustard seeds, cumin seeds, and fenugreek seeds. Let them splutter.
- Add turmeric powder, red chili powder, chopped green chilies, ginger-garlic paste, and curry leaves to the pot. Sauté for 1-2 minutes.
- Pour the whisked yogurt-besan mixture into the pot. Stir continuously to avoid lumps.
- Add water and salt to the pot. Bring the mixture to a boil, then reduce the heat and let it simmer for 20-25 minutes, stirring occasionally. The kadhi should thicken and develop a rich flavor.

Prepare Pakoras:

- In a bowl, combine besan, carom seeds, turmeric powder, red chili powder, and salt.
- Gradually add water to the mixture, stirring continuously, until you achieve a thick batter.
- Heat vegetable oil in a deep fryer or a pan.
- Drop spoonfuls of the batter into the hot oil to make pakoras. Fry until they are golden brown and crisp. Remove them and place on a paper towel to absorb excess oil.

Tempering:

- In a small pan, heat ghee or vegetable oil over medium heat.
- Add mustard seeds, cumin seeds, dried red chilies, and asafoetida. Let them splutter.

Combine Kadhi and Pakoras:

- Add the prepared tempering to the simmering kadhi.
- Gently add the fried pakoras to the kadhi.
- Simmer for an additional 5-7 minutes to allow the flavors to meld.
- Adjust salt and spice levels according to taste.

Serve:

- Serve Punjabi Kadhi Pakora hot with steamed rice or chapati.

Garnish with fresh coriander leaves.

Enjoy the delightful combination of tangy kadhi and crispy pakoras in this classic Punjabi dish!

Mutton Curry

Ingredients:

- 500g mutton, cut into pieces
- 2 onions, finely chopped
- 2 tomatoes, chopped
- 1/4 cup vegetable oil
- 1 tablespoon ginger-garlic paste
- 1 teaspoon cumin seeds
- 2 bay leaves
- 4-5 cloves
- 4-5 green cardamom pods
- 2-3 black cardamom pods
- 1 cinnamon stick
- 1 teaspoon turmeric powder
- 2 teaspoons red chili powder (adjust to taste)
- 1 tablespoon coriander powder
- 1/2 teaspoon garam masala
- Salt to taste
- Fresh coriander leaves for garnish

Instructions:

In a heavy-bottomed pan, heat vegetable oil over medium heat. Add cumin seeds and let them splutter.
Add finely chopped onions to the pan and sauté until they become golden brown.
Stir in ginger-garlic paste and sauté for an additional 1-2 minutes until the raw smell disappears.
Add chopped tomatoes to the pan and cook until they become soft and the oil starts to separate.
Mix in turmeric powder, red chili powder, coriander powder, and salt. Sauté the spices for 2-3 minutes.
Add mutton pieces to the pan and brown them on all sides.
Pour in enough water to cover the mutton pieces. Bring it to a boil.
Reduce the heat, cover the pan, and let the mutton simmer until it becomes tender. This may take 1-2 hours, depending on the meat.

In a separate pan, heat a little oil and add cloves, green cardamom pods, black cardamom pods, bay leaves, and a cinnamon stick. Sauté for a minute to release the aroma.

Add this tempering to the simmering mutton curry.

Once the mutton is cooked and the gravy has thickened, sprinkle garam masala over the curry. Adjust salt and spice levels according to taste.

Garnish with fresh coriander leaves.

Serve the Mutton Curry hot with steamed rice, naan, or roti for a delicious and satisfying meal. Enjoy the rich and robust flavors of this classic dish!

Kerala Style Paneer Roast

Ingredients:

- 250g paneer, cut into cubes
- 2 onions, thinly sliced
- 1 tomato, chopped
- 1/2 cup bell peppers, thinly sliced (optional)
- 2 green chilies, sliced
- 1 tablespoon ginger-garlic paste
- 1 teaspoon red chili powder
- 1/2 teaspoon turmeric powder
- 1 teaspoon coriander powder
- 1/2 teaspoon garam masala
- 1 sprig curry leaves
- 2 tablespoons coconut oil
- Salt to taste
- Fresh coriander leaves for garnish

Instructions:

Heat coconut oil in a pan over medium heat.
Add sliced onions and curry leaves. Sauté until the onions turn golden brown.
Add ginger-garlic paste and sliced green chilies. Sauté for 1-2 minutes until the raw smell disappears.
Add chopped tomatoes and cook until they become soft.
Mix in red chili powder, turmeric powder, coriander powder, and salt. Sauté the spices for 2-3 minutes.
Add paneer cubes and bell peppers (if using) to the pan. Stir well to coat the paneer with the masala.
Cook for an additional 5-7 minutes, stirring occasionally, until the paneer is well-cooked and absorbs the flavors.
Sprinkle garam masala over the paneer and mix well.
Garnish with fresh coriander leaves.
Serve hot as a side dish with rice or Indian bread.

This Kerala Style Paneer Roast offers a flavorful and mildly spicy preparation that showcases the distinctive taste of Kerala cuisine. Adjust the spice levels according to your preference.

Aloo Posto (Potatoes in Poppy Seed Paste)

Ingredients:

- 4 medium-sized potatoes, peeled and diced
- 3 tablespoons poppy seeds (posto)
- 2-3 green chilies, chopped
- 1/2 teaspoon turmeric powder
- 1 teaspoon mustard oil (or any cooking oil)
- 1 teaspoon mustard seeds
- 1-2 dried red chilies (optional)
- A pinch of asafoetida (hing)
- Salt to taste
- Fresh coriander leaves for garnish (optional)

Instructions:

Soak poppy seeds in water for at least 2 hours or overnight. Drain the water. Grind the soaked poppy seeds along with chopped green chilies to form a smooth paste. Add a little water if needed.
Heat mustard oil (or any cooking oil) in a pan over medium heat.
Add mustard seeds to the hot oil. Once they splutter, add dried red chilies and a pinch of asafoetida (hing).
Add diced potatoes to the pan. Sprinkle turmeric powder and salt. Mix well.
Cover the pan and let the potatoes cook on low to medium heat until they are almost tender. Stir occasionally to avoid sticking.
Once the potatoes are almost cooked, add the poppy seed paste to the pan. Mix thoroughly to coat the potatoes with the paste.
Cook for an additional 5-7 minutes until the potatoes are fully cooked, and the poppy seed paste blends well.
Adjust salt and spice levels according to your taste.
Garnish with fresh coriander leaves if desired.
Serve Aloo Posto hot with steamed rice or Indian bread.

Aloo Posto is a delightful dish that highlights the unique flavor of poppy seeds and the simplicity of Bengali cuisine. Enjoy this comforting potato preparation with its rich and nutty taste.

www.ingramcontent.com/pod-product-compliance
Lightning Source LLC
LaVergne TN
LVHW081604060526
838201LV00054B/2066